So Many Dogs In My Bed

A Poetic Dog Memoir

Barbara Barth

BookLeaf Publishing

India | USA | UK

Made with ❤ on the BookLeaf Publishing Platform

www.bookleafpub.in

www.bookleafpub.com

Dedication

To all dog lovers (or pet lovers, we are all one!).
Perhaps some of my dog stories will relate to yours.
And to all the folks that work endlessly to care
for and find homes for animals in need. They have
bought me all my fur babies.

Preface

Poems are new to me, so I'm giving this my best. Just as writing was new to me when I lost my husband in 2008. But I managed to do it, a widow memoir followed by more books, self-published, finding a creative path that also included dogs, more dogs than I thought I should. In nine months, a house full of adult pups. With no one to say no, I said YES in all caps. To dogs, to life, to pushing forward through doubt and fear. My musings available on Amazon and Instagram. At seventy-six, I've slowed down or I've learned to *just be,* at home, with the dogs, time with friends. On the Board of an Art Center that keeps me on my toes, the kindred spirits I crave. Slowing down only means I give myself time to rest. Naps with dogs no longer a guilty pleasure, but quallity time with my pack. My bucket list is simple, create more, love more, give back more.

https://www.amazon.com/stores/Barbara-Barth/author/B0049M0IXO

https://www.instagram.com/barbarabarthstudio/

Acknowledgements

A big thank you to BookLeaf Publishing and their 21 Day Writing Challenge. They gave me the courage to spread my wings and try something new again. Poetry. This has been so much fun. I now brag *I'm a poet and I know it.* In all seriousness, it is a wonderful feeling to create. I do it for pleasure (just as with my paintings) and if someone finds what I do inspiring, that is more than I can wish.

1. Why I Write

Writing about my dogs, memories saved
The reason I wrote my widow memoir
Years ago, to remember what was.
My mind gets hazy, and time confuses,
We forget feelings of joy, love, fear
New experiences that blot out the past.
How comforting the written word, to revisit
That was me, that was us, my silly dogs
So many dogs over sixteen years.
My poems capturing them forever
As I recall each little touch, nudge, kiss.
So many personalities, some long gone
Still a bed full of pups to write about.
My brain reels as my fingers type
Their never-ending love stories.

2. Sleeping With Dogs

Once there was a man
Who crossed the rainbow bridge,
I like to think that we go
Where our dogs go in the end.
Life changes and how to move on
A question always asked.
Two dogs and still an empty house,
On the computer one eve a face
Popped up, a dog face, adopt me.
A link took me to a rescue site
And that was the beginning
Of my healing with dogs.
Dogs with sad stories I'll never know
A shy pup, a wild pup, an old dog,
A small dog, a sick dog, a dog too ugly
Alone, sad, discarded, no answer why.
They were me, I was them,
We'd find our way together.
Sixteen years now, so many dogs
Five to six a constant number
New dogs as old dogs pass
Dogs never live long enough.
From big dogs to Chihuahuas
They all sleep in my bed

Contented sighs, snoring so loud
Me, pushed to the mattress edge
Clinging my quilt, don't fall off,
Their comfort over mine
A truth all dog lovers share.

3. Six-Pack

How many dogs are too many
Before you're labeled
Crazy dog lady, hoarder,
Or just "You don't need
Another dog," from friends?
How many dogs can you
Love at one time without your
Other dogs being jealous?
Are you a two-timer with
Limited lap space?
How do you know your number?
I found my answer while writing,
Six. Branding important.
I love my Margaritas,
But live with a six-pack at home,
Not stopping there, a business card
Writer With Dogs to hand out,
On a roll, I bought the dot.com.
From hoarder to entrepreneur
As I talk about writing and my dogs
"How clever of you," dialog changed.
Truth be told, it's all a front,
An excuse to fool others
Get more dogs without eyebrows

Raised and criticism tossed.
I *am* that crazy dog lady,
And those that know me well. . .
KNOW.

4. Foxy-Lady

Boy Dog was gone, our first couple dog
My husband's first dog ever, a gangly pup
Malamute mix that became ninety pounds
Of devotion, his spirit dog, irreplaceable.
Yet here we were, in the dark of night
Walking into an unknown carport, grieving
Cash in hand to buy a pup on Craig's List.
A seven-week German Shepherd tiny girl
"She'll be big, seventy pounds, you'll see."
A rebound dog so we could breathe.
My husband named her Foxy-Lady
After his favorite Jimi Hendrix song.
It took a few months for them to bond,
He'd dance holding her spinning old LPs
The tall guy with the small dog dangling
Fifty pounds at best, such a feminine gal.
A large dog finally joined our home
Jake, a stray, eighty-pound pure Shepherd,
But my husband took no notice of his size,
His heart belonged to Foxy, ever faithful
To a dog with a rock n' roll name.

5. Bray

Bray, the first dog on my adoption spree
Jake was gone and just Foxy now,
My fear surfaced, what if I lost her?
One dog, never enough, no safety net
Paranoid, reeling from too many changes.
Meet Bray, my local rescue posted
A black Afghan mix, scared of his shadow,
A year to socialize him, to calm him
So they could reach in his crate
Without his pooping at human touch,
Now ready for his forever home, me.
The park was quiet, an open field
Surrounded by a circle of tall trees
Foxy's paws on the window, tail wagging
I leashed her up and we stepped out.
Bray so handsome, black waving fur
A long narrow face with ears to match
Fifty pounds of anxiety, close to panic
Trying to act normal, but brown almond
Shaped eyes told the truth, avoiding us.
The rescue girl held him tight on his lead
Then a miracle happened, Foxy took over
By his side, sniffing him, relaxing him
As no human could that day, or later.

I reached out gently, but he pulled back
Still I knew he needed me, I needed him.
At home he bonded with Foxy, trusting
Following her, a constant companion.
The day Bray shared a kiss, a day of joy
His black tongue darting out, licking
My hand, then backing off as quickly.
Everyone loved his gentle soul
Everyone wanted to win him over,
Only surrounded by other dogs
Would he allow physical contact
And it was reason to celebrate!
Always an enigma, holding back,
His ghosts never completely gone.
Bray lived his best life, a long life
On his terms, never pushed to do more
Then he could, accepted for who he was
Loved until the end, Bray being Bray.

6. Annabelle

Two dogs were not enough, never enough,
I'm in my multiples phase, time to adopt again.
If one is good, two better, or three, or more
Petfinder a place to discover true love
Better than Match for men, canines preferred.
Meet Annabelle, a grumpy, pudgy, tan cocker,
Her face in a frown, jowls sagging, hard life.
We had our meeting, I almost said no
So much prettier in her photo than person
And there I was judging her lack of beauty
Try her, you'll see, I had to agree, out of guilt.
She strutted into my house as if she owned it
Her belly low from years of birth, jiggling
That night she made her move to my bed
How that old lady jumped up I'll never know.
When I eased in under my quilt, she rolled up
Pressed that plump, warm, body next to me,
My arms encircled her, we snuggled together
Finally the best sleep in months for us both
My grumpy faced gal bloomed into a beauty.

7. Queen Chloe

The first Chihuahua that owned me
Found at a pet store dog adoption.
My mother visiting in town, a treat
We were going thrifting at Goodwill
Until sidetracked by cages next door.
"Dogs, let's look." Mother's crazy, too
Two widows that can't say no.
Amongst all the big dogs, a tiny gal
Tan, smooth coat, sitting with a lady
Is it you? The queen wants to go home.
I swear if dogs could talk, she spoke.
Enchanted by her size and beauty
"Is she available?" I prayed a yes.
"Chloe. Two years old. Owner surrender."
She handed me the paperwork and pen
Within an hour, adopted, Chloe was home
Mother and me, both grabbing for her
"You first." Mother would be gone tomorrow
And I'd have this charmer to myself.
Chloe became Alpha that day
As a Chihuahua feels is their right
The others accepted her gladly.
A fashionista I bought dresses for her

A leopard frock with a red ruffle
Chloe's signature piece, her favorite.
She lost vision that last year
Being blind didn't slow her down
I still see her face turned upward,
Eyes clouded, searching for
What she couldn't see but smelled
Dinner time, it's about time, tail wagging
Pushing into the others, unstoppable.
Her last day, I knew it was here
Something so horribly wrong
She didn't know me, I didn't
Know myself, shaking with fear.
Twelve years by my side, my heart.
Three years and a few new dogs later
I still can't believe she's gone,
Her leopard dress, fresh and clean
Hanging in the laundry room
As if waiting for Chloe's return.

8. Two Dogs In One Week

I saw them both on Petfinder late at night
From the same rescue, both black and white
Markings on their bodies, but oh so different.
Rascal and April, one is the loneliest number
But two, more than I could handle, I thought.
Rascal, a tomboy of a girl, thirty pounds of silly
One blue eye, one brown, staring at me online
Her round body, short legs, feet splayed out
Like a ballerina ready to do a pile, dance on.
And April, a hunting dog, fifty pounds of shyness
Liver spotted body, dark face, brooding eyes.
Rascal came home with me the next day,
The pack not happy with the latest, but accepting.
Still, April haunted me, those eyes, sadness
Not friendly, the Rescue said, *not adoptable.*
I went back the following Saturday and saw her
Cowering in her crate, ignoring all that passed
Yes, I'll take her, I knew she had to be mine.
She kept her distance from the others
Staring from across the room, afraid to join in.
One evening she slowly approached me,
Her nose hitting my elbow, *I'm here* she said.
She needed to feel special, to have a dream
What if I changed her name, something fancy

April became *Miss April in Paris* that night
I talked to her about The City of Lights
Her head cocked, listening, knowing
She'd been signaled out from the other dogs.
A thump of a tail, eyes bright, she bloomed
A bit of attention made all the difference
From rescue dog to Diva, a story I love to tell.

9. Chihuahua Love

Loving Chihuahuas was a big surprise
From, *I love big dogs and cannot lie*
To that small package, bag of attitude
That won me over in a heartbeat.
The image of a yapping, snapping,
Don't mess with me kind of dog
Not always true, personalities unique.
This Mexican dog, the smallest pure-bred
Loyal, bold and protective, a Velcro dog
Wants all your attention, still biting your hand.
Or barking until your head may explode,
Such a vicious sound from a small frame
If you were that tiny in a world so large,
Might you not bark, too? Not of fear
But being bold, never an underdog
I am Chihuahua, hear me roar!
Stubborn, bossy, sweetness, too
Curled up on your lap, under a quilt
I love you eyes melt your heart
Tiny but mighty, I am a slave to their love.

10. Odette

Sweet, but oh so stubborn
Easier to get a mule to listen.
Odette moves as she pleases
She's earned her freedom
From backyard breeding
Trapped in a crate, no hope.
At eight, a grandma over pups
Covered in dirt, mud on paws
Only a bath revealed her
Paler shade of white.
I met her on a lovely Saturday
The parking lot full of cars
As I weave my way to pet shop
Was it six years ago?
Crated now, but differently
Just waiting to meet me
An angel of a Chihuahua
Sparkling white fur, demure,
My heart melts again
There is room at the inn.
At home she meets her kind
A happy mingle, she fits right in
Feisty now, feeling her place,
Letting you know when it's enough

A turn of her head, a snap, *go.*
Still, she sleeps with the others
Curled, a white fur ball in bed.
As the years have passed
Her will has strengthened
A deaf ear to anything said,
She does a happy prance
To get her way, unrelenting.
Her voice like a small child
Chatting words no one knows
She stirs up the other four,
A mob scene now I can't control
Dinner? Yes, at your command.
No rest for the weary
All dogs sleep in my bed
An early riser, Odette, not me
She sits and stares, intense
Eyes wide open, never blinking
Get up, get up, get up.
It's a losing battle, and I obey
She's the boss, telling me when,
Even on my lap, on and off
Distracting me from my reading
Or I miss the end of a mystery.
She can do whatever she pleases
It's always in a gentle way, but
NO is not in her vocabulary

If I tried she wouldn't listen
She's trained me well I think.

17

11. A Dog Named Studly

They called him Chico and kept him
In a cat carrier all day into the night
A tiny male Chihuahua, seven pounds
Of soft white fur, at eight years old
His life had come to this, no one loved him.
An owner surrender I drove an hour
Steering wheel held tight, heart racing
Traffic and fear a terrible combination.
I put his crate on the passenger seat
As we eyed each other suspiciously
That moment of truth when reality hits
The drive home uneventful, quiet, sad
My small chatter went unnoticed
He had no interest in me, confused.
And then the turning point, a surprise
When he met Chloe in her ruffled dress
And fell in love at first sight with her,
Cupid's arrow straight to his heart
Filled with desire, watching eyes wide
And that silly grin males get when smitten.
She had no interest and made it known
The meaner she was, the more he persisted
(Note to self: Play hard to get if dating
Dog lesson learned loud and clear).

Eventually he won her over, the two a pair
Sleeping side by side on my lap, ah romance
My heart took flight at the sight of them
Until...
This charmer flirted with the other gals
Big Bertha, trailing behind her every step
And Sweet Odette liked to share his bed
All dogs fixed, still a mating dance,
Was my Romeo dog a dirty old man?
From Chico to Studly, the new name fit
He won my heart with his flirtatious ways
And I his, letting him do as he pleased.
Both Studly and Chloe are gone now
Within a month of each other they faded.
I'll always remember a stud of a dog
And how he made all the gals smile
Knowing romance was just a sniff away.

12. Dumb and Dumber

Is it cruel to nickname your pups
Dumb and Dumber?
A splash of humor at their silliness
The bonded pair, father and son,
Moe and Happy Dog
Delivered to my front door
From two hours away.
Watch how you comment
On Facebook late at night
A writer friend posted
Abandoned dogs need home
Anything possible at 2 AM
I'll take them, I messaged back
See you at noon, a quick reply.
Morning came, what have I done?
My panic real, but quickly swayed
The boys arrived, so scared,
My heart went out to them.
Father smaller, son tall, deer-like
Within days, their antics started
A teen rebelling against his dad
They fight, mouthing each other
Never biting, but growling loudly
Then it stops, Father protective

Cleaning son's ears licking his face
Good boy, Father loves you.
They answer now to all their names
Dumb and Dumber, smarter than you think.

13. The Christmas Gift

Our Christmas on track again
The tree sparkling with lights
Dancing to the Four Tops
Singing to my new dog
Sugar Pie, Honey Bunch
I wonder if she knows how
Much I love her?
Can't help myself
She saved our Christmas.
Three weeks earlier, spirits high
Joyfully hugging all dogs
The last big one Bertha,
Eighty pounds of naughty and nice
Suddenly passed away, unexpected
In a blink of an eye, joy to despair.
December, how could I go on
Celebrate, enjoy, the others too
Missing her, a huge empty space.
Gloom hanging heavy, sitting
At the computer, searching for
I don't know what, salvation
A dog face, black as night, appeared.
Long hair Chihuahua for adoption
Bring me home for Christmas

I filled out the forms and prayed.
Saturday took forever to arrive
I held her close, my fingers through
Her long raven hair, ears like Dumbo
Brown eyes trusting me, love in bloom
Yes! I handed the fee and got her papers
On top her name, holiday perfection
Sugar-Pie, Sugar-Pie, my mind in harmony
Driving home I sang to her
Do you know how much I'll love you.

14. Carmella

THAT Chihuahua. You know,
The one that bites, yips, barks,
THE ONE that seems typical
Of a bad Chihuahua stereotype.
As if there are any bad dogs,
But there are yappers, growlers
That are verbal every second
Hearing every noise outside.
Carmella is THAT Chihuahua
A mixed bag of aggression and love.
Seven pounds of ruling class
Teeth bared protecting my lap
Teetering over the edge of my thigh
"I'm here, get lost," to the others.
Her intake papers said it all
Does not get along with other dogs.
Can't be plainer than that, you think?
But I couldn't ignore her, pathetic
Shaking in the large pen, this tiny girl
Hunched over, tail tucked under her
Cinnamon colored smooth body
No idea why she's there from a
Warm bed to a cold cement floor.
Did she know her owner passed on?

Family dumped her at six years old.
Her head looked up as I looked in
Our eyes met, pleading, *Save me*.
Joyful in the car on the drive home
Jumping, tail on super speed, kissing
And then she met the other four.
Her rule of terror began over them.
Two years later she's learned to share,
 Not always, but better, surprising
If you believe, love conquers all.

15. Four Seasons

Winter, Spring, Summer, Fall
Never a favorite, each full of magic
And seasons with dogs more fun.
Winter, with snow on the ground
Lightly sprinkled, powdered sugar
The pups romp across the yard
A family of five Chihuahuas now
Pawprints zigzagging, noses cold.
Spring comes, gentle breezes, flowers
Dogs aware of nature, sniffing, rolling
Sitting faces up, taking in the sun
Bees buzzing close, please don't sting.
Summer, hot as hades, too much for me,
Yet dogs, panting, tails wagging, enjoy
Until a summer shower brings them in.
Fall follows bringing color, leaves drop
Brittle on the ground as dogs' paws
Snap, Crackle and Pop as they walk.
The air brisk, perfect for cuddling,
How lucky am I, discovering the wonders
Of nature through the eyes of my dogs.

16. Storm

I know the rain is coming
Before a drop has fallen.
My barometer for weather,
Two dogs' ears on alert,
Pitched straight up,
Listening, quietly, intently.
Do You Hear What I Hear?
No, my loves, but I trust their
Prickly, fur weathervanes
One hundred percent accurate.
Listen up, Weather Channel,
Dogs for hire, their radar built in.
Moe and Happy Dog, yard dogs
Living outside in all weather.
Even now, safe, warm, inside
Can't stop the fear that builds
Shaking, terrified, on autopilot.
They run, vanish, gone dogs
Under the sofa, under the bed.
Only when the storm has passed
Two dogs appear from nowhere
Good boys, they come to my lap,
For now, their world is safe again.

17. After The Rain

It's late afternoon, the storm has passed
Sun high in the sky, dapples of light
Reflecting off damp leaves from the rain.
An impressionistic painting, brushstrokes
Highlighting Salvia and Roses in vivid red,
Velvety brow soil under rich green shrubs.
Sunlight glistening across the damp grass,
A gentle breeze, tree tops swaying, dancing
To earth's music, a calm after the downpour.
I step out to the cement patio still damp
Underneath my bare feet, cool, dirty
The dogs follow, nervously behind me,
Noses upward, smelling freshly cleaned air
"Go, go run," I smile at them, convincing.
They race down the few steps to the yard,
Tails wagging, jumping, playing, until enough
House dogs only, they bound back up
We head inside, I slowly close the doors
Once last look at nature's finest work.

18. Morning

Carmella jumped up on the bed, crying
Scurrying across my chest, waking me
Her head pressed against my neck
A tiny tan paw with its dark nails held high.
Seven pounds of Chihuahua shaking, pitiful
What had she done in the wee hours?
It's okay, sweetie. Do my words comfort?
Gently, I reach and touch her front leg
She screams, snarls, and bites my fingers,
Her head pushes into my hand, a perfect fit.
A drama queen, this little one, not the first time
But always I worry, is it real, is she hurt?
So small, so fragile, I take her seriously.
I get up, she jumps off the bed, paw high
The other pups follow to the kitchen
Still dark outside, but they want breakfast
There's no turning back, I feed them.
Carmella dances in circles, paws on floor
I've been played again, outsmarted, she's fine.
The gal knows how to work me, relieved, happy
Coffee made, *Life Is Better With Dogs* mug in hand,
Too awake to go back to bed, I check my emails
The dogs are sleeping in their beds now, quiet
Just me and my laptop, morning has begun.

19. Patio View

Sitting on the small cement patio
Air heavy with gardenia sweetness,
The overgrown bush ripe with blooms
Branches leaning on my prize roses
I should trim it, but I like it wild.
Pristine gardens not my style
Or am I just lazy, I'll never tell.
Intoxitated by the heavenly scent
I watch the dogs' short legs running
Through freshly mowed grass
A must-do with little dogs that
Can disappear in tall blades.
Noses sniffing at the ground,
Finding delight in unseen smells
What treasures have they found?
Worth rolling on, oh my, serious stuff.
Mission accomplished, they move
To different corners of the fenced yard,
Heads raised, taking in the warmth,
Chihuahuas worshipping their sun.
Closing my eyes, I lean back in my white
Victorian garden chair, comfortable,
Content, happy, sharing garden delights
With my pack of small Chihuahuas.

20. Night Moves

I'm content now with quiet nights, sitting in my
Leather wing chair, not worried about the tear a
Small dog's nails made it in last month, or last year,
I can't remember, what I remember is the joy
The pup had scratching on the chair, anxious to
Jump up and twirl, flopping like a round dough ball
Smack in the middle of my lap, licking my hand.
Sometimes I look out the French doors, fairy lights
Dancing across the top of the chain link fence
I let the dogs out into the yard, watching as they
Disappear into shadows then reappear in moonlight
Running wild in the confines of a small, fenced area.
Dashing back into the den, their adventure over
A biscuit for them, some chips and soda for me.
Back in my wing chair, feet propped on a foot stool
A small patchwork quilt tossed over my legs,
I have so much to do, but choose to do nothing.
Curled up in our usual spots, sighs all around
Looking at five small dogs, I smile
Nothing is important except the moment
Sharing an evening in the company of my dogs.

21. Paint Party

I've been writing like crazy
Today, I need to paint
On canvas, colors and joy
Brushes, acrylics, free spirit.
Time is lost when I work
Hours pass, I'm in my zone
My workspace simple, my desk
So the dogs can be near.
You should see the mess,
Paint splatters everywhere
Even a dollop on Odette's head.
I fling colors on canvas, I'm fast
The joy of it coming together
 Still amazes me that I can do it
And like the images that appear.
I paint for me, what I love
Using ice cream colors
The cherry on top, when
Someone admires my work.
As a new widow I wanted
To find a creative path
Sixteen years later,
Dogs and art, my lovely life.

www.ingramcontent.com/pod-product-compliance
Lightning Source LLC
LaVergne TN
LVHW010833200726
843508LV00012B/2583